IT Manager Career Secrets

Tips And Techniques That IT Managers Can Use In Order To Have A Successful Career

"Practical, proven techniques that will help you to manage your IT Manager career successfully"

Dr. Jim Anderson

Published by:
Blue Elephant Consulting
Tampa, Florida

Copyright © 2013 by Dr. Jim Anderson

All rights reserved. No part of this book may be reproduced of transmitted in any form or by any means, electronic or mechanical, including photocopying, recording or by any information storage and retrieval system without written permission of the publisher, except for inclusion of brief quotations in a review.

Printed in the United States of America

Library of Congress Control Number: 2013920396

ISBN-13: 978-1493695560

ISBN-10: 1493695568

Warning – Disclaimer

The purpose of this book is to educate and entertain. This book does not promise or guarantee that anyone following the ideas, tips, suggestions, techniques or strategies will be successful. The author, publisher and distributor(s) shall have neither liability nor responsibility to anyone with respect to any loss or damage caused, or alleged to be caused, directly or indirectly by the information contained in this book.

Other Books By The Author

Product Management

- How To Have A Successful Product Manager Career: The Things That You Need To Be Doing TODAY In Order To Have A Successful Product Manager Career

- Product Manager Product Success: How to keep your product on track and make it become a success

Public Speaking

- Secrets To Planning The Perfect Speech

- Secrets To Organizing The Perfect Speech: How to organize the best speech of your life!

CIO Skills

- CIO Business Skills: How CIOs can work effectively with the rest of the company!

- Managing Your CIO Career: Steps That CIOs Have To Take In Order To Have A Long And Successful Career

IT Manager Skills

- IT Manager Budgeting Skills

Negotiating

- Preparing For Your Next Negotiation: What You Need To Do BEFORE A Negotiation Starts In Order To Get The Best Possible Deal

Miscellaneous

- Power Distribution Unit (PDU) Secrets: What Everyone Who Works In A Data Center Needs To Know!

- Making The Jump: How To Land Your Dream Job When You Get Out Of College!

Acknowledgements

Any book like this one is the result of years of real-world work experience. In my over 25 years of working for 7 different firms, I have met countless fantastic people and I've been mentored by some truly exceptional ones. Although I've probably forgotten some of the people who made me the person that I am today, here is my attempt to finally give them the recognition that they so truly deserve:

- Thomas P. Anderson
- Art Puett
- Bobbi Marshall
- Bob Boggs

Dr. Jim Anderson

This book is dedicated to my wife Lori. None of this would have been possible without her love and support.

Thanks for the best 21 years of my life (so far)...!

Table Of Contents

IT MANAGERS HAVE SOMETHING ELSE TO MANAGE: THEIR CAREERS! 8

ABOUT THE AUTHOR 10

CHAPTER 1: EMPLOYEE MOTIVATION: WHAT TO DO WHEN YOU FEEL PASSED OVER 14

CHAPTER 2: WHAT MAKES A JOB THE PERFECT IT JOB? 18

CHAPTER 3: BUT I WANT TO WORK 80 HOURS A WEEK…! 21

CHAPTER 4: NEUROSCIENCE CAN MAKE YOU A BETTER IT LEADER ..25

CHAPTER 5: IT MANAGEMENT CHALLENGE: BREAKING IN A NEW BOSS 28

CHAPTER 6: WHAT IS AN IT LEADER TO DO WHEN WINNING IS EVERYTHING? 32

CHAPTER 7: 5 STEPS TO HELP AN IT MANAGER FIND A MENTOR 35

CHAPTER 8: HOW IT MANAGERS CAN MAKE TIME WORK FOR THEM 38

CHAPTER 9: HOW CAN AN IT MANAGER GET AHEAD AT YOUR COMPANY? 42

CHAPTER 10: PIMP MY IT JOB! 46

CHAPTER 11: SO HOW DO YOU GRACEFULLY LEAVE AN IT JOB? 49

CHAPTER 12: IT EMPLOYEE MOTIVATION: FIXES ARE MORE IMPORTANT THAN PROBLEMS 52

IT Managers Have Something Else To Manage: Their Careers!

It's not easy being an IT manager. There are constant staffing issue, budget issues, project issues, and the challenge of keeping your management informed about what is going on. The one thing that too many of us end up overlooking as we try to accomplish all of these things is that we have one more management job to do: manage our careers.

It can be all too easy to forget about actively managing your IT manager career. In fact, some of us make a conscious decision that we're not going to spend any time on it – we'll just let things take care of themselves.

It turns out that this can be one of the worst decisions that you'll ever make. For you see, if you ignore your IT manager career, there is a very good chance that everyone else will ignore it also. Time will pass and one day you'll look around and discover that you are right where you were a long time ago – nothing has changed!

Instead, take charge of your career! How fast your career advances will be based on your personal performance and how well your team performs. In order to manage your career, you are going to have to take charge of both of these items.

The good news is that it's not all that hard to do. There are several steps, like finding a mentor, which will speed you on your way to your next promotion. Take your time and carefully read each of the chapters in this book to get hints on what steps you need to start taking today in order to take charge of your career.

Keep in mind that in this whole entire world, you are the person who is the most interested in you being successful. That means that you need to step up and accept responsibility for your career. Invest the time and I'm sure that you are going to be very pleased with the results that you are able to achieve!

For more information on what it takes to be a great IT manager, check out my blog, The Accidental IT Leader, at:

http//www.TheAccidentalITLeader.com

Good luck!

- Dr. Jim Anderson, November, 2013

About The Author

I must confess that I never set out to be a CIO. When I went to school, I studied Computer Science and thought that I'd get a nice job programming and that would be that. Well, at least part of that plan worked out!

My first job was working for Boeing on their F/A-18 fighter jet program. I spent my days programming fighter jet software in assembly language and I loved it. The U.S. government decided to save some money and went looking for other countries to sell this plane to. This put me into an unfamiliar role: I started to meet with foreign military officials and I ended up having to manage groups of engineers who were working on international projects.

Time moved on and so did I. I found myself working for Siemens, the big German telecommunications company. They were making phone switches and selling them to the seven U.S. phone companies. The problem was that the switches were too complicated. Customers couldn't tell the difference between one complicated phone switch from another complicated phone switch. Once again I found myself working with the sales and marketing teams to find ways to make the great technology that the engineers had developed understandable to both internal and external customers.

I've spent over 25 years working as an senior IT professional for both big companies and startups. This has given me an opportunity to learn what it takes to manage and IT department in ways that allow it to maximize its output while becoming a valuable part of the overall company.

I now live in Tampa Florida where I spend my time managing my consulting business, Blue Elephant Consulting, teaching college courses at the University of South Florida, and traveling to work with companies like yours to share the knowledge that I have about how to create and manage successful IT departments.

I'm always available to answer questions and I can be reached at:

Dr. Jim Anderson
Blue Elephant Consulting
Email: jim@BlueElephantConsulting.com
Facebook: http://goo.gl/1TVoK
Web: http://www.BlueElephantConsulting.com/

"Unforgettable communication skills that will set your ideas free…"

Create IT Teams That Are Productive And A Valuable Asset To The Rest Of The Company !

Dr. Jim Anderson is available to provide training and coaching on the topics that are the most important to people who have to manage IT teams: how can I build a productive IT team (and keep it together) while at the same time delivering high quality projects on time ?

Dr. Anderson believes that in order to both learn and remember what he says, speakers need to laugh. Each one of his speeches is full of fun and humor so that what he says "sticks" with everyone.

Dr. Anderson's IT Manager Skills Training Includes:

1. How to identify and attract the right type of IT workers to your IT team.

2. How to request, manage, and track your IT budget

3. How to stay on top of changing technology and security issues so that your team is always using the right tools?

Dr. Jim Anderson works with over 100 customers per year. To invite Dr. Anderson to work with you, contact him at:

Phone: 813-418-6970 or
Email: jim@BlueElephantConsulting.com

Speaking. Negotiating. Managing. Marketing.

Chapter 1

Employee Motivation: What To Do When You Feel Passed Over

Chapter 1: Employee Motivation: What To Do When You Feel Passed Over

I recently had a chance to talk with a friend of mine who works as a developer in the information technology department for a major telecommunications firm. I was surprised to discover that he was very angry and was thinking about quitting his job. It turns out that he had just completed a major project. He and two others had put in those non-stop 60-70 hour days. He had been away from home for the better part of two months and he was very proud of what was finally produced.

However, what had gotten him angry was that two other individuals had joined the project late in the game, had not worked nearly as hard as the core group of three had, and in the end they not only got credit for the project's success, but they also got promotions while the core group of three were not promoted. Is it any wonder that my friend was so angry?

We spend a lot of time recruiting the best information technology employees and then we spend at least as much time worrying about employee motivation all too often only to end up with angry, bitter staff. In the case of my friend, what had gone wrong was instantly clear to me because I've done it to myself countless time. I call this situation, the "engineering field of dreams" problem.

Jobs in Information Technology allow us to focus on building things using only our minds and hands (for typing). As engineers we have a bad habit of completely focusing on solving the technical problem that we've been assigned and not lifting our heads up until we have a finished product. The problem with this is that we then expect the rest of the world to look at what we've made and realize what a great worker we are. In my case, I blame my Mom because whenever I took something that I had made to her she always reacted with joy and surprise and told me that it was the best thing that she had ever seen. Unfortunately, the rest of the world doesn't work that way.

So what should my friend have done? While he was working on the project he should have realized that he had another job to do at the same time. In IT management speak we'd call this an "overlay job". Every single day he needed to be managing his career — thinking about what he needed to be doing in order to get recognized for what he was doing and get considered for a promotion the next time an opening showed up.

You know what he said when I told him this: "Hey Jim, I just don't like to brag about myself!" Two quick replies to that: (1) if you don't, then who do you think will? and (2) bragging would be bad, informing others would be good.

I ended up having a very long talk with my friend; however, here is the gist of what we talked about. He needs to identify who he needs to make aware of his contributions (his boss, his bosses boss, and the bosses of any department that his project interfaces with). He needs to communicate with these people regularly (Monday, Wednesday, and Friday).

Communicating does not mean sending them mindless status reports. He needs to send brief, concise emails that provide valuable information such as "We had a problem, but here is how we solved it…" When he sends an email to these important people, he needs to address it to only them — don't CC them or send it to a distro list. One-to-one sends a powerful message.

Finally, he needs to do more than just send emails: he needs face time with the decision makers. I suggested that he use the excuse of "checking to make sure that you agree with the decisions that we've made" line to set up a meeting.

So remember: you are in charge of your career and nobody else. As technical professionals we all suffer from a "love my work, love me" syndrome and we need to do a better job of communicating with those in charge in order to move our career along.

Chapter 2

What Makes A Job The Perfect IT Job?

Chapter 2: What Makes A Job The Perfect IT Job?

Sorry in advance for going off on a bit of a rant here, but I've become fed up with both IT workers and managers who continue to completely miss the boat when it comes to creating, working, and managing exciting and fulfilling IT jobs.

This time my trigger was going out to lunch with a group of my friends who have gotten themselves roped into running one of those internal "High Achiever" IT management programs. You know the type: your boss identifies you as having management potential and so you get picked to attend a weekly/monthly class where they teach you about teamwork and, perhaps, introduce you to other parts of the company.

This particular program selects the team to run next year's program from the students who are participating in this year's program. My friends had participated in last year's program and were now complaining about how much of their time running this year's program was taking up and that they didn't feel that they were getting anything out of it.

I didn't actually reach across the lunch table and grab them by their shirt collars; however, I was sorely tempted to do so. My frustration with them came from the simple fact that they were not taking the time to notice that they had been given a once-in-a-lifetime opportunity.

I asked them how many management training courses their company had sent them to. The answer was, of course, none. I then proceeded to point out to them that what they were doing as a part of running this training course was basically real-world practice for becoming IT directors, executive directors, VPs, etc.

The challenge was that none of the students in the class worked for them. This meant that they couldn't get things done by telling people what to do (managing), instead they were going to have to convince folks to do what they wanted them to do (leadership). This was where the real learning for them was going to take place!

At the end of our lunch, my friends were reinvigorated and pumped up about what they now had to accomplish. Their job had not changed one bit, but the way that they looked at their job had undergone a complete transformation.

At the end of the day this is the key to making any IT job a success: you have to clearly identify the challenges that it will be required to solve and the acknowledgments that will be given for solving those challenges. This is exactly what IT staffers are looking for in a job and they will stay if they find it and move on if they don't.

What really got my goat was trying to understand where my friends' managers were in all of this? Instead of having to go out to lunch with me to get re-focused and re-energized, their managers should have been doing this on an almost daily basis.

Once again it appears as though IT managers have allowed themselves to get too focused on project schedules, code delivery, and server configurations and have missed the key role of IT management: creating challenges and providing acknowledgments. How good of a job are you doing at this?

Chapter 3

But I WANT To Work 80 Hours A Week...!

Chapter 3: But I WANT To Work 80 Hours A Week...!

Over the past weekend I got a call from Phil who is one of my long-time colleagues who works in the telecommunications business. We got to talking and then, as it always does, the macho game of "who's working harder" came up.

This around Phil won the game: he had just put in 105 hours in the past week. I had worked hard, but I didn't even come close to that – remember, I'm a big believer in completing the most tasks, not spending the most time.

You just know that I couldn't be a graceful loser, so I followed up with some questions about how the rest of his life was going. Initially he said that things had never been better; however, after some probing on my part he started giving up the goods: his personal life was a wreck.

His troubles seemed to fall into two main categories – personal health and love life. Phil is about 5"8' or so and, last time I saw him, had a fairly lean frame. On the phone he told me that in the last three years he's put on about 25 extra pounds. This has done bad things to his health as well as making a difficult home life even rougher.

I remembered Phil's wife as being gorgeous and very nice. However, Phil confided in me that because of the stress in their relationship, she had been gaining weight also. Additionally, she was fed up with him for never being around to help out with the kids.

In the IT field, this "love of work" or "work as a gigantic black hole" syndrome can swallow us up at any time. What's interesting is that by hunting around on the Internet, I found an article by Kelley Holland that said that this is a relatively recent occurrence.

The folks over at the National Bureau of Economic Research keep records on this type of stuff and they say that back in 1983 the lowest paid workers worked the most. However, by 2002, the highest paid workers were 2x as likely to work longer hours as the lowest paid ones.

Why do we do this to ourselves? It turns out that the old Puritan work ethic seems to be alive and well and working in IT. It seems as though since we are being well paid for our work (are you?) we feel the need to work more.

Additionally, we seem to like our jobs more than other people do. Finally, now that we don't HAVE to work 12 hour days in the mill, maybe we are more willing to do in order to maintain our conspicuous consumption lifestyle.

What's the downside for IT workers? Stand up & look down at your shoes. If you can't see your shoes, then you know what's going on here. Early days require a stop at some drive through on the way in and late nights often involve a run to the food machine at the end of the hall.

There's no reason to wonder why we are getting bigger! Toss in the fact that we're getting too little sleep and we try to make up for this by multitasking which by now everyone should know is a really, really bad idea. Click — now you have a snapshot of Phil's life.

What to do? I talked for a little while longer with Phil and asked him, now that he had set a new personal record for hours worked in a week, how he was going to fix his life? Phil said that he had started taking fruit with him to work and eating that instead of worshiping at the powered doughnut cathedral at the end of the hall.

He had also started to take the stairs at work more often and tried to go out for a walk at lunch time. He was cutting back on work by leaving on time on Friday and having a set time to work on email on Saturday and was trying very hard (but currently failing) to go unconnected and do no work on Sunday.

Chapter 4

Neuroscience Can Make You A Better IT Leader

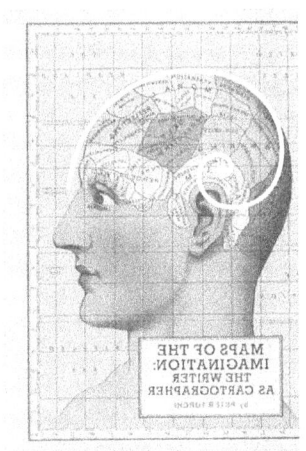

Chapter 4: Neuroscience Can Make You A Better IT Leader

Dr. John Median is a developmental molecular biologist who recently sat down with the Harvard Business Review and had a talk about what we've recently found out about how the brain works and what this can tell us about being better IT leaders.

The key question that IT leaders want to get an answer to is to find how relevant neuroscience discoveries are to the day-to-day job of management. Dr. Median says that he thinks that one of the reasons that we are all so fascinated by brain research these days is because it truly is the most interesting and complicated processing tool that we have ever seen.

How's this for a fascinating fact: there are as many neurons in your brain as there are stars in a typical galaxy. Despite having this level of knowledge about the brain, we still know very little that can be related to the real world.

One thing that science has learned is that stress is very, very bad for our brains. Since it hurts our brains, it also decreases our productivity. The reasoning behind this is pretty simple.

Evolution has wired our brains to help us to survive. What this means in practical terms is that our brains were originally set up to deal with stress for short periods of time: 30-60 seconds. Remember "fight or flight?" However, in today's modern IT workplace everyone is under stress almost all the time. Our brains were never set up to deal with stress all the time. This can lead to other problems with things like a lack of motivation, poor sleep and immune system issues.

So what happens when we have too much stress in our lives? Dr. Median says that stress can mess with our hormones. When this happens, the connections between brain cells that help us remember things can start to fray and weaken.

Unfortunately, the hormones associated with stress seem to like to prey on the part of the brain that is called the hippocampus - where our memories are kept. Some studies have guessed that the total cost of lost productivity due to stress is somewhere around $200 billion/year. What does this mean for IT managers? Simply put, anything that you can do to lower the stress level that is being experienced by your team will pay back rich dividends.

One very interesting point that Dr.Median makes is that our memory is NOT like a Xerox machine. Our brains and our memory were always designed to help with one thing only: our survival. We really have no idea HOW we remember things, but what we do know is that it seems to take a long time for memories to become permanent.

The best way to remember something is to constantly re-expose yourself to it. Once again. for IT managers this means that if you want your team to remember the company's mission statement, then you're going to have to start every meeting off by reading it to the team.

The good news out of all of this is that our brains will continue to grow and change throughout our entire lives. If you want to have a better shot at having a healthy, growing brain for your entire career, then the #1 thing that you've got to do is to exercise.

Exercise in any form and aerobic exercise in particular helps your brain. Dr. Median points out that people who exercise are 50% less likely to get Alzheimer's disease. From an IT leader point-of-view, this goes along nicely with the idea that a healthy team is a more productive team. Anything that you can do to make it easier for your team to stay in top shape will once again help your team to perform that much better.

Chapter 5

IT Management Challenge: Breaking In A New Boss

Chapter 5: IT Management Challenge: Breaking In A New Boss

A great deal has been written on how IT workers can deal with getting a new boss. For that matter, a lot has been written on what you need to do if you become the boss of a collection of IT workers. Shucks, I've even written a lot about how to find out what your CIO wants you to do.

However, what's been missing (up until now) is what an IT manager should do if he/she gets a new boss. The challenge here is that it's not just you that will be evaluated by the new boss as they go about setting up shop, but rather it will be your team that the new boss will be evaluating. What's an IT manager to do?

Let's get something out of the way first. As an IT manager your new boss can broadly be placed into one of three categories: fantastic & almost god-like, average, and horrible tyrant. If your new boss falls into the fantastic / tyrant buckets, then you've got a whole other set of issues. However, since most bosses fall into the "average" bucket, let's spent our time talking about what to do with just this type.

There are some interesting questions about why you have a new boss in the first place – what happened to your old boss? Oh, and by the way, why didn't YOU get your old bosses job instead of this new person? Once again, just to keep things simple let's push those items off to the side for now. Let's assume that you've never met your new boss before – the hardest scenario.

It can appear to be a daunting task if you try to determine how to win you new boss' favor before you meet them. In today's era of a distributed workforce, there's a good chance that you and your new boss may not be in the same town. This means that meeting them face-to-face should be one of your highest priorities. No matter how good you are at email or how engaging you may be over the phone, there is no substitute for a face-to-face meeting in order to allow your new boss to size you up. Travel to meet them or have them come visit you.

When you meet them, what will you talk about? The key here is to let them do most of the talking. Your value to your new boss rests on the type and quantity of problems that you can make go away. It really is that simple. The worst situation that you can find yourself in is if your team is in charge of solving problems that your new boss doesn't really view as being problems! This is why it's critical for you to let your new boss tell you what he/she thinks their most important problems are.

Remember the first day of school back in elementary school? Everyone in class was trying to show off for the teacher so that they would gain her affection from the get-go. Things are very similar when you get a new boss, everyone will be trying to get on his/her good side starting on day one.

You can improve your odds of doing this if you take a moment and think like a chess master. Your new boss is dealing with exactly the same issues that you are – he/she desperately wants to "look good" for their boss who put them in this new position. Your long-term value will be in what you and your team can do to make your new boss look good to his/her boss.

So what DON'T you want to do when you have a new boss? Probably the worst thing in the world you can do is to overwhelm them. Email is easy to send and all too often IT managers start to CC their new boss on every email to show the boss how important the IT manager is.

A much better approach is to show your value by creating a condensed summary of what your team is currently working on. Even here there are some dangers: us IT managers like to list each and every little accomplishment so much so that our summary often turns out to be equivalent to "War & Peace" in length.

Keep it short – one computer screen of information should do the trick. Write it in such a way that your new boss now has useful information that they could pass on to their boss.

The rough rule-of-thumb is that a new manager has about 90 days to show his/her stuff. You need to be tracking these first 90 days and doing everything that you and your team can to make your new boss shine in that time. Investing in your new boss now will result in a rich payout later on…

Chapter 6

What Is An IT Leader To Do When Winning Is EVERYTHING?

Chapter 6: What Is An IT Leader To Do When Winning Is EVERYTHING?

So here's an interesting issue that I'm sure that most CIO's and IT managers would love to have: how best to manage over-the-top "A-Type" personalities? Hey, we all know folks like this (put that mirror down!) These are the people in our company / department / team for which winning can become more important than the big picture. We all seek to have enthusiastic people on our teams, but what can we do when enthusiasm turns into something very, very bad?

So what's the real problem with really wanting to win a discussion, a bidding war, or a design decision? Simple – focusing too much on winning can cause smart people to make bad decision errors. When IT managers and executives become overcome by competition, they can shift their goals from maximizing value to beating their competition at any cost.

Dr. Deepak Malhotra has done a great deal of study on such folks, and he spilled his guts in an article that he wrote for the Harvard Business Review. What he found, is that there is very strong evidence that, what he likes to call "competitive arousal", is at the root of a number of high profile business mistakes. IT is not immune to this effect.

Now this brings up a very good point: there is nothing wrong with wanting to win! We all enjoy winning, hey – it makes us feel good. In fact, we are often willing to pay a price to win. Just to make sure that we all understand it, there is often a good reason to want to win.

We encounter competitive situations in which we want to win in all sorts of different forms: auctions, negotiations, legal issues, merges, acquisitions, promotions, or even when we go recruiting new talent. In some of these cases, it may be worth it to end up paying more than the fair value for what we really, really want because it will weaken our competition, etc.

Here's the trick: if you are going to go after some prize with that much zeal, then you had better have done an upfront analysis of the situation and determined what your limits of loss that are acceptable are. Additionally, you are going to have to balance these against the benefits to your IT organization.

If you don't do this BEFORE you get involved in the competition, and you try to do it DURING the competition then that's when your competitive arousal will end up overriding your rational decision making process.

So what's an IT leader to do? You are going to have to develop a way to identify what causes this competitive arousal to show up. Once you can spot it, you are going to need to avoid or at least reduce the possibility that it will screw-up your IT department's strategy or destroy your department's value. Keep an eye on how competitive you are feeling and make the right decisions when your competitive arousal is high.

Chapter 7

---

5 Steps To Help An IT Manager Find A Mentor

Chapter 7: 5 Steps To Help An IT Manager Find A Mentor

Mentoring is sorta like that networking thing. You know that it's probably a good thing to be doing. However, you're not quite sure how to get started with it and so it seems to always end up on your "should do" list where, of course, it never gets done.

Whenever you read about someone's success in business, they always seem to give credit to their mentor. Man, I guess having a mentor can help one succeed in business, I really should get one of those...

A traditional mentoring relationship was when an older colleague would talk a younger colleague under their wing and they would show you the ropes and maybe even open some doors for you along the way. Bad news: those days are pretty much over at this point in time.

Today mentors need their own mentors in order to keep up with all the changes that are occurring in technology, globalization, workplace diversity, etc. Since the old way of mentoring is now officially broken, IT managers need a new way of getting the guidance that mentoring used to provide.

A clever solution to this problem is to not limit yourself to one mentor, instead develop a small network of mentors – each having a particular area of specialty. Keep in mind that mentors for this "personal board of directors" do not need to come from where you work: professional societies, university, friends, all are potential candidates. Here are 5 steps that will help you build your mentor network:

1. **First Look In The Mirror:** How can you ask others to help you unless you know what kind of career help you need? Spending time listing out your strengths and weaknesses is the best way to decide what kind of mentors you need.

2. **Determine What Your Needs Are:** Once you know what your strengths and weaknesses are, then you are ready to decide what steps you need to take in order to achieve your goal. If you want to be CIO, then you probably need to first be a Director, next an Executive Director, and so on. Knowing this type of information will help you to understand what types of mentors can give you the coaching that you'll need in order to get promoted.

3. **Pick Your Mentors:** Instead of waiting around for a kindly Sr. Executive to reach out and offer to coach you (just like in the movies), you need to select those whom you will invite to be your mentors. Remember that mentoring has to be a two way street so make sure that you have something to give back to the people that you ask to mentor you.

4. **Weed & Sow Constantly:** As time goes by, your mentoring needs will change. This means that you need to be constantly re-evaluating who is currently in your mentoring network. Over time your needs will change and you will need to gracefully swap out board members.

5. **Give More Than You Receive:** Keep in mind that mentoring is a two-way street. Ultimately you will want to be sought out by others to be their mentor so that you can learn from the best and the brightest. The only way to make sure that this happens is to develop a reputation for being a great mentor yourself.

Chapter 8

How IT Managers Can Make Time Work For Them

Chapter 8: How IT Managers Can Make Time Work For Them

Just where does the time seem to go? I don't know about you but as of late I seem to be running out of time or just simply running behind more often than in the past. I'd like to blame the current turmoil in the financial markets; however, that's not the problem.

There are many, many more people who are better qualified than I talk about time management (I'm sorta a fan of GTD myself), but I do have one secret that I'd like to share with you. No promises, but if you believe what I'm going to share with you and if you take the time to implement it, then there is a pretty good chance that you'll become the best IT manager in the world. Sound interesting? Then read on…

If you think back a bit, you might remember that there was a book called The Secret that was very popular a while ago. In a nutshell, the secret was that if you can imagine something, then you can make it happen.

This applies to making others believe that you have control over your time. However, I'm going get just a bit more specific here and give you one single change that if you implement it will have a dramatic and positive impact on your life: start showing up early.

What this means in the day-to-day life of a IT manager is that you need to start to show up for meeting early (5-10 minutes will do) and even more importantly, you need to start to jump on call bridges early (5 minutes will do here).

I don't know about you, but up until just recently I was a constantly late shower-upper. I would slide into calls 5 minutes late and hope that whoever was running the meeting would not stop the call and ask who had just joined when they heard the "beep" that announced my arrival. I'd slug through the call and then slink off when it was over no better or worse for the time spent on the call.

A few weeks ago, I accidentally showed up for a call early. You can imagine how surprised I was when there was nobody on the bridge when I joined (there was that moment where I felt that I needed to check to make sure that I had the right call-in numbers). What happened next really caught my attention: other people started to join.

These just happened to be people that I had been trying with no luck to get in touch with. I had very quick, very short conversations with three of them as they joined and got commitments from them to send me answers and materials that I desperately needed. As others joined I exchanged small talk with them and reconnected with people that I knew but had not seen in a long time.

When the call's leader joined he fumbled around for a bit and this gave me time to ask a very good, penetrating question about what he wanted to accomplish on this call and that got everyone involved in a discussion. Man, it was almost like I was running the show!

Based on the success of this accidental event, I started showing up early for all of my meetings that week and found that the same sequence of events repeated itself. Others looked at me as though I was in charge, I connected with other people who were in the meeting, and I was able to make face-to-face requests for support and materials that were never turned down. Wow – who knew that getting what you wanted could be so easy?

Yes, I realize that showing up early for meetings and calls won't solve all of life's problems. However, it sure seems to make a lot of little things run much easier. When you couple that with the fact that it's so very easy to do, why not give it a try and see what it does for you?

Chapter 9

How Can An IT Manager Get Ahead At Your Company?

Chapter 9: How Can An IT Manager Get Ahead At Your Company?

If we agree to take a step back from the world of IT for just a moment, how about if we spend just a bit of time talking about your career. How's it going? Are you where you'd like to be right now? Perhaps more importantly, have you been seeing your peers do better than you lately?

Us IT Managers are generally pretty good at the technical side of doing our jobs; however, when it comes to managing our careers we are all too often just a bit clueless. Good news, some smart folks have been thinking about this problem and they have some suggestions to help us...

Geoff Colvin has written a great book called **Talent Is Overrated** in which he talks about just what it takes to be successful. He's got some good news for us and some bad news. Which would you like first?

Let's start with the good news. All too often we tend to think that genetics plays a large role in somebody's success. In sports we have Tiger Woods, Michael Jordan, Lance Armstrong (ok, maybe that's not the best example!) and in business we have Jack Welsh, Richard Branson, and even Warren Buffet. Clearly all of these folks must have come from amazing genetic stock, right?

Colvin throws this idea out the door. Yes, sports superstars probably do have some natural talents that help them during their career; however, that's not what made them a superstar.

In business, if you've ever seen pictures of the really BIG names, then you'd quickly understand that they don't LOOK like they are anything special. However, Colvin says that great performance (from which comes great success) basically rests on one specific action more than anything else: deliberate practice.

Let's be real clear what is meant by practice here. We're not talking about going out and hitting 2,000 golf balls on a practice tee and then declaring that you are as good as Tiger Woods. We're not talking about hosting and running 1,000 business meetings and then telling the world that you have Sir Richard Branson's leadership skills.

Nope, what we are really talking about is practicing with a focus. This means that you hit a ball / run a meeting and at the end you sit back and ask yourself "…what could I have done better?" You then make a change in how you hit a ball / run a meeting and then you do it again. You ask the same question at the end of the activity and repeat it over and over again. Just in case you are missing this subtle point: this is no fun to do whatsoever. However it is necessary if you want to be better.

Colvin pointed out two great examples of people who have done just exactly this and gone on to greatness. The first is Jerry Rice who was an NFL wide receiver who wasn't really all that big nor was he really all that fast (in comparison to the other wide receivers on the field with him). However, Jerry noticed that by the end of a football game, all of the players on the other team were totally exhausted.

Jerry spent the time focused on one thing: building up his endurance. What this meant is that when everyone else had nothing left to give, he had an extraordinary advantage over them during the final 15 minutes in the game. He used this advantage to score, score, score.

Colvin also talks about the comedian Chris Rock. Chris is a huge star and puts on shows in large stadiums. However, long before those shows, he spends months going from small comedy club to smaller comedy club in order to practice new material and refine, refine, refine his act.

Here's some of the bad news: Colvin believes in something called the "10-year rule". What this means is that he believes that it can take 10-years to achieve a high level of excellence in just about any field.

However, you can still do it. What it will take is deliberate practice. Two key activities are called for here: over practicing and getting feedback from others. One final point: Colvin says that if your job feels easy, then you are unlikely to ever become a star. Words to think about...

Chapter 10

Pimp My IT Job!

Chapter 10: Pimp My IT Job!

What to do when you are stuck working on a program/project that is not the executives' current favorite? Do you feel as though you are stuck in your company's technical back waters and that your skills are growing older, staler, and more out-of-date each and every work day? Do you look enviously at your coworkers who are working on more glamorous projects and using cool new tools like Ruby or various Web 2.0 toolkits to create shiny new beasts?

Well fear not, amazingly enough you are not alone. Most of the IT community is in your shoes — we work to keep the critical systems up and running and try to make them just a bit better each and every release. "Project Envy" is a fact of life that we all live with. What to do about it?

There is no single magic cure for this affliction; however, here are three ways that I have dealt with this in both my own career and in trying to keep folks on my team motivated:

1. **I.N.T.L.S: "It's Not The Language, Stupid":** Lots of times our jealousy of other workers and projects stems from the fact that they get to use a neat new toy that we don't get to use. Get over it — good design is good design, no matter what language or tool you have to work with.

   Back in the day, folks were able to get FORTRAN to do some pretty amazing things that it had never been originally designed to do. Think about it this way: how boring must it be if the language / tool that you are using to solve a design problem does too much of the work for you. Instead, focus on creating the tightest, clearest code that is humanly possible. We all like a challenge and this will help you to overcome language envy.

2. **Can Anyone Say "Soft Skills?":** If you find yourself trapped on a back waters project, instead of spending

your days surfing dice.com, how about if you spend some time working on those skills that you are going to need in order to make it through your entire 45 year career? Skills like communication, delegation, negotiation, etc. If your career eventually takes off, you will desperately need these skills so use this "pit stop project" as an opportunity to bone up on what you'll need.

3. **Play the Metrics Game**: Most IT departments have fallen in love with metrics and this offers you a great way to get some department wide recognition no matter what project you find yourself stuck on. Back water projects are generally in charge of older, stable applications or systems. You can use this to your advantage.

    Study what metrics your department is tracking and determine which of them are most important to upper level management. Then take a look at your project and ask yourself how you can make this project #1 in terms of department metrics. By doing so you'll rise to the top and will get noticed. This just might be enough to get you moved to another more popular project.

There are many more things that you can do should you find yourself stuck on a project that turns out to not be the flavor-of-the-week. Complaining, sulking, and surfing for a new job are always options, but there are much better ways to spend your time!

Chapter 11

So How Do You Gracefully Leave An IT Job?

Chapter 11: So How Do You Gracefully Leave An IT Job?

In the world of IT we seem to spend a lot of time talking about downsizing and folks getting fired. What hasn't really been discussed is what the best way to leave a job is. Although in my younger days I was very good at burning my bridges behind me, these days I've come to realize that this is in fact a very poor long term strategy.

When I left my first IT job after 6 years in basically the same position for a job at a different company in a different town, I had no experience in how to break off the relationship. This very large company had a policy that you would sit down with someone from HR on your way out the door and ask you several questions.

These questions dealt with issues like where are you going, why are you leaving us, and what suggestions would you like to leave us with that would improve how we do things. What I didn't realize at the time (ah, how young we once were) was that the real reason for an exit interview is to determine if the firm is going to be sued by a disgruntled employee. Pretty much everything else that you say is nice, may be noted, but really doesn't matter.

Seeing as most firms don't know how to handle the fact that you are leaving, what's an IT worker to do? First, you need to realize that once you announce that you are leaving the company, everything instantly changes. Some firms will show you the door immediately. Others will give you two weeks to wrap things up, but you will instantly be treated as an outsider.

Even if you are willing to work at full force for those last two weeks, you are now officially a "short timer" and nobody really wants to work with you anymore. What this means is that if there is anything that you really need to hand off or wrap up, you should do it BEFORE you announce that you are going to be leaving.

This is always tricky to do because your close team members may start to guess that something is up. You can handle this in two ways: lie, or tell them that you are considering some offers but have not yet made up your mind. Lying is never a good idea even if it seems like the easy way out — the truth always comes out eventually. Slowing introducing everyone to the idea that you might/are leaving seems to allow everyone time to come to grips with it.

The new job that you are planning on leaving your current firm for probably looks like the best job in the world: great cube, great people, fabulous pay, undreamed of perks, etc. Please note: the last thing in the world that you want to do is to tell everyone about these reasons for your leaving.

No matter how good a teammate they were, this will make them turn green with envy and that is never a good thing. I've always found that telling everyone that I felt that I had completed what I had joined the firm to do and that the new firm had offered me a challenge that I just couldn't pass up seems to satisfy most folks and does not produce a great deal of ill will.

I guess that it goes without saying that in the world of IT there is always a good chance that you'll be working again with some of the folks that you are leaving. Yet another reason to leave on good terms!

Chapter 12

IT Employee Motivation: Fixes Are More Important Than Problems

Chapter 12: IT Employee Motivation: Fixes Are More Important Than Problems

The engineer in all of us can rise up and take over whenever a problem shows up. In the world of information technology, when either ourselves or one of our staff screw up, personnel issues can get shoved aside as we focus on finding a solution to the problem at hand.

However, if you can take a step back for just a moment, you'll find that this is a rare opportunity to define your career. In this day and age in which IT employee retention is so important, the ability to pause can be critical.

We all make mistakes and the same goes for those who either work for us or work on our team. When somebody really makes a mistake, the whole world seems to come to a screeching halt when both the problem and the person who caused it are finally identified. What you do next will define how everything turns out. You've got a bunch of options:

- **Don't Go Bi-Polar**: All of us tend to favor an extreme reaction when we realize that a mistake has happened. Either we blow our top and insist that someone else is responsible or we get very embarrassed and think "Oh no, I really screwed up this time." Both reactions are the wrong response — instead, take a step back to evaluate the situation and keep calm even if that is the hardest thing in the world to do.

- **Plan, Plan, Plan**: don't ignore the problem. And yes, you should probably tell your boss about it so that he hears it from you and not someone else. Be sure that you accept responsibility (I mean, what else can you do?) and make sure that you have a plan for what to do next BEFORE you tell him.

- **Don't Point Fingers of Blame**: Focus on finding a solution to the problem instead of focusing on the source of the problem. One key aspect of IT jobs is that we seem remember and reward the heroes who fix problems and we rarely seem to remember how the problems happened in the first place. This is your time to shine!

- **Find A Problem Mentor**: If ever there was a time in your career to find someone to talk to about your situation this is it. Keep in mind that they may not be in your office and may not even work for your company. Find them, explain the situation, and seek their guidance as to what you should be doing next.

- **Say That You Are Sorry**: Amazingly enough, this may be the perfect time for you to simply say "I'm sorry". A sincere apology may be the hardest thing in the world for you to do; however, it may act like a sudden rain storm over a forest fire. If an apology is not appropriate or needed, then at least state how you feel "This is a bad situation and I'd like to help correct it" and then move on.

We have all made mistakes in our career and we will probably make even bigger ones as we move forward. However, it's how we react to these mistakes that really defines who we are.

Hard work does not guarantee success. However, success does not happen without hard work.

— Dr. Jim Anderson

Create IT Teams That Are Productive And A Valuable Asset To The Rest Of The Company !

Dr. Jim Anderson is available to provide training and coaching on the topics that are the most important to people who have to manage IT teams: how can I build a productive IT team (and keep it together) while at the same time delivering high quality projects on time ?

Dr. Anderson believes that in order to both learn and remember what he says, speakers need to laugh. Each one of his speeches is full of fun and humor so that what he says "sticks" with everyone.

Dr. Anderson's IT Manager Skills Training Includes:

4. How to identify and attract the right type of IT workers to your IT team.

5. How to request, manage, and track your IT budget

6. How to stay on top of changing technology and security issues so that your team is always using the right tools?

Dr. Jim Anderson works with over 100 customers per year. To invite Dr. Anderson to work with you, contact him at:

Phone: 813-418-6970 or
Email: jim@BlueElephantConsulting.com

Photo Credits:

Cover - By: Public Affairs
http://www.flickr.com/photos/losangelesdistrict/

Chapter 1 - By: Roland Gesthuizen
http://www.flickr.com/photos/plakboek/

Chapter 2 - By: Province of British Columbia
http://www.flickr.com/photos/bcgovphotos/

Chapter 3 - By: bark
http://www.flickr.com/photos/barkbud/

Chapter 4 - By: hawkexpress
http://www.flickr.com/photos/hawkexpress/

Chapter 5 - By: Ahmad Hashim
http://www.flickr.com/photos/3ammo/

Chapter 6 - By: Sigvard.Alarcon
http://www.flickr.com/photos/zevonbrowne/

Chapter 7 - By: Keri-Lee Beasley
http://www.flickr.com/photos/klbeasley/

Chapter 8 - By: Andrea Zamboni
http://www.flickr.com/photos/zamboniandrea/

Chapter 9 - By: Charles Dyer
http://www.flickr.com/photos/charliedees/

Chapter 10 - By: Larry Kang
http://www.flickr.com/photos/kang/

Chapter 11 - By: id iom
http://www.flickr.com/photos/id-iom/

Chapter 12 - By: MOVband UK
http://www.flickr.com/photos/movbanduk/

www.ingramcontent.com/pod-product-compliance
Lightning Source LLC
Chambersburg PA
CBHW071820170526
45167CB00003B/1384